Leading Others into the Presence of God

A Worship Leader's Guide

Chris Park

Curate, St James and Emmanuel, Didsbury

GROVE BOOKS LIMITED

RIDLEY HALL RD CAMBRIDGE CB3 9HU

Contents

Acknowledgments

I would like to thank the Revd Chris Puckrin and Revd David White for their pastoral wisdom, inspiration and courageous leadership, all those who have shared this amazing journey with me in St Michael Le Belfrey too numerous to mention, and especially my wife Angela—my biggest fan and fiercest critic, for all her love and support.

The Cover Illustration depicts Christ on the cross tearing open the veil of the temple, and is © Richard Coates 1996

First Impression October 2004
ISSN 1470-8531
ISBN 1 85174 576 9

Introduction 1

Hunger for God is the foundational motivation for any worshipper.

I grew up in both Anglo-Catholic and Anglican Evangelical circles and moving into the charismatic has been quite an adventure! There are many reasons why I moved, but mainly I found a hunger for God that I had not known previously. This hunger meant that I longed to meet with him and be filled with him more than ever before. Worship is not about styles of music, spoken liturgy, or even sound doctrine. The question is, have we got the hunger for Jesus?

Worship is about a journey. We travel from where we are into God's presence in a way which is quite distinct. Here our hunger is satisfied and yet we long for more. This is worship in which the direction of the dialogue is towards God for a sustained period of time, which we can think of as a graph with the appearance of a wave which reaches a climax.

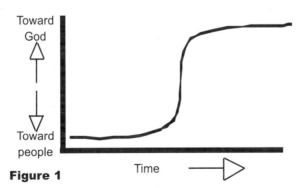

Figure 1

It might seem simplistic to plot the shape of a service in this way, but it is a really helpful exercise if we are to consider the ways we are leading people into God's presence.

Figure 2 gives my impression of my experience of worship before I moved into the charismatic. I attended each week and I learned and received a lot, but it felt more like snacking than feasting. The dialogue was directed to the people, then to God, then to the people, then to God and so on.

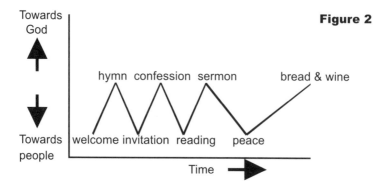

Figure 2

It is this sense of journey that captures the utterly extraordinary privilege of charismatic worship. It is our honour day by day to journey into the Lord's presence and feed with him. In Christ we are called to journey from the omnipresence of God to the manifest presence of God, from the experience of God as he is in all places to the experience of his particular presence here. This can happen in the big top of a convention, in 'St Boris in the Wardrobe' with old Mrs Scroggins on the organ, in a small group or alone as you worship on a Monday morning.

In this booklet we explore this journey. What is a worship journey? *Why* should we make it? *How* do we make it? How can we lead others on it? However, the most important thing of all is that we make the journey ourselves. There is no more important place to be than in his presence.

> I sought the Lord, and he answered me; he delivered me from all my fears. Those who look on him are radiant... (Psalm 34.4–5a)

As we practise this particular journey we must remember that 'worship' has a wider meaning. Paul tells us that our whole life is to be an offering of worship (Romans 12.2). This is important because it reminds us that what we are discussing here is one element of our overall worship, a vital element, but not the whole of our discipleship.

Questions for Reflection

1. What 'shape' is the worship at a typical service that you lead? Draw a graph of your own—which of the graphs above does it more resemble?
2. How flexible is your 'liturgy' to be used to build a focus towards God?
3. Could you plan your next service on this graph?

What is the Worship Journey? 2

There are different models of a worship journey.[1]

My primary model is based on the image of heaven in Revelation 4.1–11 which we will use as our example in this text. Here John describes an open door into heaven, which leads to a throne upon which God is seated. So we begin our worship journey outside the door, enter through and come before the throne joining all of heaven in the praise of God. We then rest before the throne. The following day we are able to discern more clearly whether we have worshipped, by looking at our lives and the lives of those we worship with. Are we more Christ-like, more fruitful? Worship is a way of life not just something we do on a Sunday.

The journey has the following stages:

- Outside the door
- Entering Heaven Through the Door
- Coming Before the Throne
- Resting before the Throne
- 'Monday Morning'

It is important to note that while I describe worship as a journey through stages, in reality it will be more flowing without obvious joins.

Our purpose as leaders of worship, no matter what the context, is to lead people to the throne of God. This is our objective and we must keep it in mind.

Resonances with Pilgrimage

One of the many reasons this model is helpful in understanding our job as we lead worship is that the idea of journeying is so popular and appealing. To talk of a worship journey resonates with our knowledge of our roots in Jewish practice as they journeyed to the temple singing Psalms of Ascents (Psalms 120–134). It draws on our instinct for pilgrimage which has been evident down through the ages and is still alive today.

It has within it the expectation that we will 'move on' or change, that we will meet with God and that the journey will be worthwhile. All three of these are vital as we lead God's people in worship, both for the worship leader in preparation and for the congregation as they worship.

The Journey is Made Possible by Christ

This journey is only possible through Christ. When he met the Samaritan woman in John 4.4–26 he was clear that the physical location of the worshipper is no longer important. The woman in the story points out that the Samaritan place of worship is Mount Gerizim and that for the Jews it was Jerusalem. Jesus responds with the verse we read in every book ever written on worship.

> Woman, believe me, the hour is coming when you will worship the Father neither on this mountain nor in Jerusalem…But the hour is coming, and is now here, when the true worshippers will worship the Father in spirit and truth, for the Father seeks such as these to worship him. (John 4.21–23)

The pilgrimage to the presence of God is no longer focussed on the temple in Jerusalem, Mount Gerezim or any other location. Jesus has ushered in a new era which is not based on temples, sacrifices and law. He has done it all by his 'one perfect and sufficient sacrifice, oblation, and satisfaction.' We read in the account of the crucifixion how just before Jesus dies, the curtain in the temple is torn in two (Luke 23.45). The barrier to the Holy of Holies has been removed. Access to the weighty presence of God has been opened up, and this is now for all nations not just the Jews and, by extension, for those outside of the Christian church today as well as those within.

The barrier to the Holy of Holies has been removed

True worshippers will worship the Father in spirit and truth. To worship is to express our love for God the Father in whatever way we find appropriate, in the light of the truth of who he is and who we are before him.

This idea of worship as a journey is helpful because it reminds us of our main aim in gathering, it directs us as we plan our worship and it rings true with our heritage. This is true whether the worship is simply between you and God or in a larger setting. As we explore this journey together we begin by focussing on the context of a worship group leading a congregation. But most of the principles we discuss can be used as an individual (see chapter 8).

Later in this booklet we will continue exploring how we actually go about leading the worship. It is necessary before we do that, though, to address some basic questions. We as leaders need a clear idea of why we worship. And we need to be brutally honest about the people that God calls us to be as we lead worship. If we lose either of these we might as well pack up our cow-bells and go home.

We as leaders need a clear idea of why we worship

Questions for Reflection

1 What are the key elements of a worship journey?

2 How would you describe the 'worship journey' which you most appreciate? Could you draw your own picture of it?

3 Using your picture or mine, how would your choice of music or other items enable others to be drawn along in the journey?

Why Make the Worship Journey?

Heaven—the Best Place To Be

The throne room of God in heaven is our eternal home. We are 'aliens and strangers' (1 Peter 2.11), 'in,' but not 'of' this world. The best is yet to be, and when we encounter the presence of God we have a taste, however small, of our eternal home. The psalmist sensed this in the temple:

> I have seen you in the sanctuary and beheld your power and glory. Because your love is better than life, my lips will glorify you. My soul is satisfied as with the richest of foods; with singing lips my mouth will praise you. (Psalm 63.2, 3, 5)

When we rest in the presence of God we are wonderfully satisfied as we experience a profound sense of his love for us. This is the place we are healed. This is the place where we have a taste of eternity. This is the place where the weary find rest. This is the place where we find the richest of foods.

We are Invited to Costly Participation

The gospel revolves around an exchange in two directions. It begins with God in his love and mercy moving towards us in Jesus. His death and resurrection bring us forgiveness and life and invite us to respond in love, obedience and worship. God reaches out in love and we are invited to respond in love. God offers himself as a sacrifice of atonement, we offer ourselves as a sacrifice of praise.

The Jews were required to bring animals to sacrifice as part of their worship. Jesus' death does away with this, but now we have the less tangible requirement of bringing the whole of our lives as an offering of worship, a sacrifice of praise. Worship must cost us something if we respond to what God has done for us. Jesus himself models this in the Garden of Gethsemane

Worship must cost us something if we respond to what God has done for us

(Mark 14.35–36). Here is Jesus laying down his life for our sakes, surely the most fundamental act of worship which Paul has in mind when he writes Romans 12. And yet Jesus wrestles with his Father because he knows how much it will cost him.

Worship is supposed to be costly, and whether that cost is large or small, material or spiritual, this dynamic must not be ignored. Often it costs families emotionally just getting to church! It costs to worship when we are suffering from physical, mental or emotional dis-ease. Singing songs of worship that celebrate God's goodness may be the last thing we want to do, but it is important to realize that this act of sacrifice is central to our act of worship, and although this might sound small in comparison with other acts of costly discipleship it is part of a discipline.

It costs us to worship when we are suffering from physical, mental or emotional dis-ease

It is not just our response to God, however, which comprises sacrificial worship. Worship is one way we engage in the spiritual battle here on earth. In the Old Testament (2 Chronicles 20.21) the army of Jehoshaphat was led into battle by the worshippers. Today's battles are not against flesh and blood, but against the spiritual forces of evil (Ephesians 6.12), but worship is still a key weapon. David Parker tells a story of one particular man who came to his church ignorant of Christ and far from God.[2] He described going to church as 'being in the presence of goodness for the first time in his life.' Satan cannot stand where Jesus is worshipped and we encounter the presence of God.

Created to Make the Worship Journey
Thirdly we worship because this is how we are made. The God who created the universe, the sparrow and the ant, created you and me in his image. As we reflect on the wonder of this, praise wells up within us, 'I praise you, for I am fearfully and wonderfully made' (Psalm 139.14a). Furthermore, being created in the image of a relational God means that we are made to be in relationship, not least with God. Such a relationship is always one of worship. It is all too evident in our society that if we do not worship God we will end up worshipping something or someone else.

Moreover, as Christians we are being re-created as Christ does his redeeming work through the Holy Spirit in us. We are marked by the Holy Spirit, (Ephesians 1.13) and 'when we cry "Abba Father" it is that very Spirit bearing witness with our spirit that we are children of God' (Romans 8.15b–16).

This is a taste of our eternal inheritance (Revelation 4.8–11). Worship is happening in heaven now and we join the angels when we worship God. There are many things that we will leave behind for ever one day, death, disease, and diets to name a few...but we will be worshipping the Almighty for eternity.

So why do we make the worship journey? Because it give us a taste of our eternal home, because this is one way we respond to God, and because as human beings we are created to worship our creator. Here we relish the feast that satisfies and yet we have a hunger for more.

Questions for Reflection

1 How can we best bring ourselves and others to reflect on why we worship?

2 Is this important, and how do we monitor it in practice?

3 How do we maintain our motivation in worship?

3 The Leaders of the Journey—
Heart Standard?

Why we worship is important, but it is also vital to consider who we are to be if we would approach God.

In one way, of course, we come 'Just as we are, without one plea' (but that of his blood). However, this is held in tension with the truth that if we will ascend the hill of the Lord, we need 'clean hands and a pure heart' (Psalm 24).

The Bible is full of references to integrity, 'for the Lord does not see as mortals see; they look on the outward appearance, but the Lord looks on the heart' (1 Samuel 16.7). This 'heart standard' is vitally important because who we are determines what we do. The heart standards for any Christian leader are holiness, prayerfulness, humility and so on. All of these are vital for a worship leader with the additional heart standard of a longing for God's presence. We see this clearly in the Psalms. 'I would rather be a doorkeeper in the house of my God, than dwell in the tents of the wicked' (Psalm 84.10).

Moses would go into the tent of meeting and speak with God (Exodus 33.9–11). Joshua would go with him, but while Moses returned to the camp, Joshua remained in the tent, lingering in the presence of God. In the long run it was Joshua and not Moses who led the people into the Promised Land. Here was a heart standard which stood him in good stead for the future.

Holiness

One of the basic duties of worship leaders is to nurture their own hidden life with Christ, and that of others they serve in the worship group.

One of the basic duties of the worship leader is to nurture their own hidden life with Christ

If you are to nurture this holiness in a worship group it does help to run the group like a 'small group' (cell group, house group, or whatever you call them in your church) and to have the same line up every week. Having people who are committed to each other and the worship of God is healthy. There is always a temptation for group members to try to skip the 'accountability' and 'fellowship' bits, either because they do not like them or do not understand their importance. It is worth considering a rule that if you cannot make the practice, you do not sing/play that week.

There was an occasion when I became so concerned about holiness in the group that I considered having three groups, two playing alternate weeks and the third looking after the local soup kitchen! We could then swap round each term. Jesus values this 'not-for-public-display' holiness and we do well to follow his example (Matthew 6.6).

Character Not Gifting

Christian character is about becoming more Christ-like. It is this character that will shape our gifts, musical or otherwise, and use them positively. We only need to read the letters to Corinth to see that people can exercise their spiritual gifts, but without character they can become destructive rather than building up the body of Christ.

Of course we need some level of musical skill in the group, but if that is all we have then we are performers or entertainers rather than worshippers— let alone worship leaders. Gifting is shallow and temporal without character. Putting people on a public stage to 'perform' worship can be destructive, and is frustrating for the congregation who can tell the difference between performance and worship. You know when a couple love each other by the way they talk to, look at and treat each other. It is the same in worship. You can tell whether someone loves Jesus by the way they sing to him.

Be discerning about your group members. What does their body language tell you? What do their eyes say to you? How do they live their lives? Character is the thing which causes people to serve in the less public places. When the worship group turn up for the half night of prayer you know that their characters are in good shape.

Being in a worship group can easily become part of our identity, rather than being secure in simply being a child of God. Worship itself then becomes an idol. We can hide behind our instrument. How do we feel when we have to lay our ministry down? We need to guard our hearts and stay pure.

Be a God Pleaser Not a People Pleaser

Sometimes people ask, 'Was the worship good tonight?' There is a risk here of reacting to people rather than God. This is a recipe for swinging from triumph to disaster; for the worship leader primary affirmation must come from God. The only way I know how to walk away satisfied from any public ministry is to prepare prayerfully and deliver what God gives me. If I sense him changing track during the service I follow him as best I can, but in the circumstances of my life I want to be sure that I have done what I believed the Lord asked of me. Then I stop trying to please people and focus on pleasing God. Here my heart standard is trust in God. Am I happy to be received by him and him alone?

Accountability Relationships

Accountability helps us to keep right relationships with God and one another. I have found a good way to develop accountability relationships is to ask some basic questions when we come together to practise:

- How is your love life with Jesus?
- What has God been doing in your life this week?
- How are your relationships with your immediate family / friends / spouse?
- Do you need to forgive someone?
- Do you need to confess to a particular sin?
- Are there any practical challenges in your life at the moment?

We then allow time to pray for each other out of the things people share. This is simple leadership of a small group, and as always leaders are included. We are there to wash feet and be as vulnerable as we can with one another. Try to allow as much time as needed for this part of the practice.

At St Thomas' Crookes in Sheffield they have developed accountability relationships into what they call 'huddles.' These are groups of leaders who come together to pray for one another and listen to one another out of the issues going on at that time in their lives. During these 'huddles' the leader uses a sheet with a number of statements and each person says which of these statements most applies to them at the present time. The whole group then pray into this.[3]

Accountability relationships encourage individuals to take responsibility for their own spiritual lives. They also build the relationships within the group as we become aware of our different needs and help each other at a practical as well as spiritual level.

Boundaries

Our world believes that freedom is the removal of boundaries so that we can do as we please. The Bible teaches that God gives us boundaries within which we are free to operate, and that this is perfect freedom. For the Christian the boundaries are no longer law, but a person, Jesus Christ. Part of our role as worship leaders is communicating boundaries to the group and ensuring that we are living within them.

Let us be practical. What do you do if a member of the worship group comes to the service dressed in a way which means that people will struggle to see beyond them to Jesus? For example, how do you handle a teenager wearing a tee shirt with an 'FCUK' logo on it? I would ask him to turn it inside out or put a jumper on. What do you do if one of the women in the group has rather too much flesh on display which would cause a distraction for many of the men in the congregation? I would ask one of the older women to sort out this type of issue, but I would indicate the need to dress more sensitively. Here the heart standard is that we want to be transparent, not a distraction, so that we might lead people to Jesus.

A second example of boundaries may concern personal integrity around sexual relationships. I believe this is about the direction people are heading and not that people are already wonderfully holy, but we do need to be clear about where we stand. There could be a time when explaining discreetly to a group of teenagers that choosing to sleep with their boyfriends and girl-friends means choosing not to be a part of the group. What we ask for is honesty and integrity on their part in their lives where only God can see what is really happening. It is often helpful for the group to agree boundaries together.

Having said all this, if we had to be perfect none of us would get anywhere. Having permission to fail, or at least a lack of condemnation when we fail, from the church leader and the worship leader is a very liberating value in a worship group. This goes for both our personal lives and our public worship. Loving acceptance when we fail in our personal lives promotes honesty and trust, and in the long run issues are dealt with rather than hidden. Permission to fail in leading worship frees us to take risks and so explore the depths of God in worship. Looking back in my own life, having permission to fail in worship has caused some spectacular mistakes, but I have known far more victories because of this freedom.

As I have said these things are important if we are serious about leading worship. We are going now to look at how we might prepare to lead worship, but in one sense we must never move on from these challenges.

Questions for Reflection

1 How do you nurture and form the hidden holiness of your group and for yourself?
2 How are you developing the characters of your team?
3 What boundaries do you lay down with your group?
4 How do you treat failure?

4

How We Make the Journey—
Choosing Songs

Returning to the metaphor of the worship journey from the door into heaven to the throne room of God, let us consider what the journey will look like in terms of song choice.

We need to choose songs, and we need to work out how they fit together. It is important to re-emphasize that while I am describing different 'stages' in the journey, in practice we do not see the joins. The worship flows from one stage to the next.

Moving Between the Stages

As worship leaders and as a whole group we can do a number of things to enable this flow.

First, we can ensure that the music works to link the songs. Note the keys you are playing in and often you can work out a 'bridge' between the songs so that the music is continuous. Sometimes you can use silence effectively, or it may be better just to stop a song before starting the next. It is usually easiest if the worship leader begins the next song, but good understanding and communication with the other group members are essential.

Good understanding and communication with the other group members are essential

Secondly, we can pray, usually in praise or thanksgiving, leading out of the songs we sing. This is part of our worship, but it also has the advantage of creating space for God to lead us.

As a group it is important to practise bridges and introductions, but we also need to be open to changes in direction if the worship leader believes that God is leading elsewhere. This may sound like a contradiction but in rehearsals we can practise being spontaneous. We can use exercises like the worship leader moving from one song to another in different keys and seeing how quickly the group are able to join in.

How, then, do we choose songs to enable the journey?

Outside the Door

This is the place where we begin. Here we can sing about God as well as to God (for example, 'Be still for the presence of the Lord,' or 'These are the days of Elijah'). The lyrical content can be more verbose and hymn-like at this place in the journey. The structure of the songs may be linear verses (rather than a repetitious verse/chorus structure). The content is primarily doctrinal, credal or affirmative.

It is important to remember that we as worship leaders may be further into the journey than this, but we should assume that those we serve begin outside the door. We pray that faith is rising up as we sing truth about God and ourselves so that our hearts are moved towards praise. This takes us to the next stage.

Entering Heaven Through the Door

As our hearts are turned towards God so we want to praise him. The words are now directed to God rather than about him (for example, 'My Jesus, my saviour,' or 'I will worship'). The tempo can be fairly upbeat as we engage in praise. Structurally the songs become more repetitive than linear and their content is primarily that of praise and declaration.

Here we are becoming aware of the awesome presence of God. This is the key moment. As worship leaders we are looking for the song or instrument which takes us through the door into heaven, which breaks the yoke and frees us to worship. This is about anointing, and we will look at this in the next chapter.

Coming Before the Throne

Now we are through the door, we come before the throne where God is seated in all his majesty. This is like Isaiah's experience: 'I saw the Lord sitting on a throne, high and lofty; and the hem of his robe filled the temple' (Isaiah 6.1b). In this place the songs can become quiet and can be devotional ('I love you Lord') expressing love and thankfulness on the one hand, or utter awe of God on the other ('You are beautiful beyond description').

At this point we might sing in tongues. Spiritually this is the place of intimacy and awe. We are in the very presence of God.

Resting Before the Throne

In this holy place before God's throne we stop and rest for as long as we are comfortable. This is a place of intimacy and receiving, of repentance and healing, of feasting and blessing and prophetic revelation. This is our home, and here is all we need, but it would be wrong to give the impression that this place is about us. It is a God-centred place, the glory is his, the praise is his, he is the centre and the focus, and this is the best place imaginable.

This stage is characterized by a minimal amount of music; usually there is a need to protect or create stillness. What a worship group does not play is as important as what it does play. One instrument playing just two chords (like a major to minor/major 7th) will enable space. Again we may sing in tongues. We may have people sing or speak out words of prophecy. If someone sings spontaneously then we can help them by accompanying them with a very simple two chord structure. If someone starts up a familiar song then we sing and play along if we can, or we can hum along if we do not know it well. It takes courage to sing out so we encourage them as best we can.

This resting can be in silence, but this is a weighty silence filled with the glorious presence of God. This is silence where you can hear a pin drop. It is not the empty silence of daydreams and distraction.

On a practical note, if you find yourself in a situation where there is singing in tongues, when this quietens down, leave space for silence. In this silence God often speaks.

Ending this time sensitively is important and can be difficult. Sometimes we simply say 'amen' and move on with the service. At other times we might sing a hymn which engages with our awe and wonder and brings us to a place where we move on in the worship, something like 'Hallelujah sing to Jesus.'

Monday Morning

Finally it is important to include the 'Monday morning' experience, that is, what happens the day after we have encountered God's immanence.

The way we tell whether or not we have worshipped is not by evaluating the service itself or the reaction of the people, but by looking at our lives the next day. Are we more fruitful? Are we more Christ-like? Are we more em-powered for service and the works of the kingdom? Has God's grace had such an impact on us that we are changed from 'glory into glory?' This is how we know whether we have worshipped. Worship is not about how many folk had their hands in the air, were slain in the Spirit or sang with renewed gusto!

There is a danger that describing the journey in this way can sound con-trived or, worse, manipulative—this is the way to meet with God; do this, and you will have a spiritual experience. But it is not about techniques; rather, I offer this journey as a framework by which we can enable people to en-counter God in a significant way. I believe it is rooted in the Bible's description of what it is like to encounter God in worship; it is true to my own experience; and as a worship leader it is a way of reflecting on what I am doing that has been effective in creating space for those I lead.

This worship journey is so life-giving to us as Christians. The key point on the journey for me is where we enter heaven, and it is anointing which enables us to make this move. How do we find it? When does God release it? These are necessary dynamics to consider if we are faithfully to lead God's people in worship.

Questions for Reflection

Think about some worship that you are planning at the moment:

1 What is the journey you propose to take?

2 What type of songs (or other material) do you need to shape that journey?

3 Can you place songs in this way into a running order, or onto a picture like mine?

---

5 How We Make the Journey— Finding the Anointing

Let me be blunt: anointing is the key.

If I am hungry for God it is no good just singing about him, I want to be with him. Getting through the door is the target and as worship leaders we are here to lead others through. That is our purpose. The theory of the worship journey is useful in helping us to understand and shape the process, but what we are seeking is anointing and sometimes all our plans change once we are in God's presence.

What is Anointing?

In the Bible anointing usually refers to the spiritually significant act of anointing with oil of either people, like Aaron and David, or the items used for worship, such as the ark of the covenant and the tent of meeting. At various places in the New Testament this has come to mean simply that someone has been touched by the Holy Spirit (see for example 2 Corinthians 1.21ff or 1 John 2.20, 27). Here I take the common modern meaning of anointing as referring to a person or activity being touched by the Spirit to bring us to God. This is an experience for which we may have different names, but it is familiar to us as practising Christians. If you are unfamiliar with anointing in worship, you may know anointing when you read the Bible and a verse or truth suddenly comes powerfully alive. There is revelation where previously there has been either ignorance or only head knowledge. Anointing is the difference between God revealing himself and him being distant. I define it as the power of the Holy Spirit working naturally in a supernatural way.[4]

In worship this anointing will often come during a particular song or during the playing of a particular instrument. The practical question is how do we discern this? The answer is prayerful practice together in the discernment of what God is doing. When I am preparing, I ask myself 'Have I got the hunger for Jesus?' Hunger for Jesus is the heart standard which enables anointing. We seek him and sometimes he anoints what we do, but if we chase the experience of anointing we get nothing. Anointing is God given. God can anoint any song, any instrument, or the voice of any worshipper. We cannot produce anointing, all we can do is prepare well, learn to recognize what God is doing among us, and respond to it.

So How Do We Prepare...As An Individual?

As worship leaders we need to look firstly at our own relationship with God. We all face the temptation to gloss over our spiritual life and simply play the role. This is both a sin and a recipe for disaster. Then we need to prayerfully choose the songs for the group practice and preferably worship with them before we meet up as a group. Play them in the car on the way to work. Use your own discernment to see where the Holy Spirit wants to bring his anointing. This all arises out of a healthy walk with God. Kevin Prosch asks 'How can you sing to someone on a Sunday you have not spent time with during the week?'[5]

...As a Group?

When you come together as a group, practise worshipping with the songs. Learn to recognize which songs move your focus from the flesh to the Spirit. Where are you getting the sense of our awesome God? Which songs are causing us to want to lift his name on high 'where the things of earth grow dim'?[6]

You need to teach people to recognize what is happening. When *you* recognize God at work ask: 'Did you sense the anointing there on that song/flute introduction/voice?' It is like learning to recognize anything; it takes someone with experience to point it out, but once you have sensed anointing, you know it, and you know when you do not have it. We know these things together in our spirits.

Worship arises from the heart where we are marked by the Holy Spirit. The main purpose of the practice is to discern where the anointing is. Arranging the songs and playing well is important, but only to the extent that it helps us worship. The battle in the congregation is invariably fought and won at the practice.

Do be aware that when it comes to the service, anointing might be on the congregation rather than members of the worship group. You can hear it rise up in the people. At this point it may be useful for the group to stop playing, and have just the voices singing, or even to have nothing at all. Join in with what God is doing and try not to get in his way. This is not about you and me. It is about him. Even Jesus said, 'the Son can only do what he sees the Father doing' (John 5.19).

Anointed Worship Takes us to a New Place

As Christians we are marked by the Holy Spirit (Eph 1.13). The Christian life is about the battle between our old nature which we need to crucify daily, and our new nature which God gives as a gift of his grace. When we move in the power of God's grace what seemed impossible becomes natural. There is a unity between the person of Christ in us, by his Spirit, and the Father in heaven. This is the territory of anointing and we should not underestimate its power.

> O thou who camest from above
> the fire celestial to impart,
> Kindle a flame of sacred love
> on the mean altar of my heart.
>
> There let it for thy glory burn
> With inextinguishable blaze,
> And trembling to its source return
> In humble prayer and fervent praise.

When God anoints worship, we can leave our agenda behind and revel in the profound presence of God knowing that he is changing, renewing and empowering us. Without anointing we might learn from our songs, we might declare truth, but we are missing out on so much.

Anointed Worship is Evangelistic

Let us not be misled into thinking that this ministry is just for Christians. The presence of God draws people. St Michael Le Belfrey is situated right in the middle of York next to the Minster. We used to practise for the evening service on the Sunday afternoon with the doors open. Tourists would come in and some would stay on for the evening service, and on at least one occasion I recall a man who came to the vicar at the end of the evening asking, 'What must I do to be saved?'

This is an area I explore further in the resources on the Grove web site (www.grovebooks.co.uk), but let me just add here that I am convinced that this means we need to take worship out of the church, on to the streets and into places where people meet.

Anointed Worship Enables Us to Lament

Neither should we think that this worship is all 'happy' or 'clappy.' If we are truly worshipping within the anointing of God all that we are comes before his throne. I am writing this booklet in July 2004 and believe that the need to lament is something of a prophetic word to the church today, not just a cognitive observation of a lack in our church worship. 'Break our hearts with the things which break your heart Jesus, that we might suffer with you as well as reign with you.'

Lament is a huge part of the Psalms, it is around us in our culture and it is notably absent from our churches. This is serious and again I explore this at greater length on the Grove web site.

Anointed Worship Leads Us in a Circle of Grace

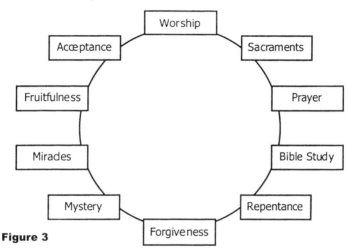

Figure 3

This anointed worship is a means of God's grace. This grace enables us to be changed from one degree of glory to the next, to live lives empowered by the Holy Spirit and see his kingdom come.

There are, of course, many other means of God's grace and they are all linked. When we encounter the presence of God we are often convicted of our need to forgive or repent. We find a greater hunger for God's word. We may experience God healing people we pray for. We may have a greater desire to receive the sacrament of the bread and wine.

This is what I call the circle of grace (figure 4). It is the opposite of a vicious circle. The more we receive of God's grace, the greater our hunger for more and the more we give away. The more we give away the more we receive.[7] Speaking as a Yorkshire man, this is paradise!

Questions for Reflection
1 Do you recognize this sense of anointing in worship?
2 How and where do you teach others to know it?
3 How often do you sense that anointing when you are leading worship?
4 How hungry are you for Jesus?
5 Where can you feast this week, and can others join you?

6   How We Make the Journey— Some Practicalities

Worship is, I believe, fundamental to church life. This means that it is bound to be under attack. We need to be very practical about how we move forward and be aware of potential problems before they arrive. We need to soak the whole enterprise in prayer, before, after and during leading worship. Here are some observations which I hope will help.

The Relationship with the Church Leader

A church leader is called to release people into ministries. How far others can go is determined by how far a church leader will let them go. A basic principle should be that it is the church leader who is in overall charge and has the final say in the case of any disagreement. But the church leader needs to push the boundaries as far as possible and give as much authority to the worship leader as that person can handle. This means that the church leader might need to learn about delegating, whilst the worship leader needs to be seen to be a responsible steward of the authority that is given. It is important that each know where the boundaries lie, and that they are able to grow in trust over a period of time. It would be good to discuss and agree issues raised in this chapter before things get heated. In particular, they need to agree on some key practical issues:

> **The volume coming out into the main body of the church via the PA system.** Agreeing some standard settings on the desk is not difficult and can save time and tension if established at an early stage.
>
> **How long will the worship group play?** In some churches this will be less of an issue than others. I suggest that you try to give at least 15–20 minutes for a specific time of sung worship in order to allow the journey to take place. In an Anglican setting this can be done by creatively using the *Service of the Word*, and I have been impressed with the flexibility of *Common Worship*.
>
> **Introducing new songs.** I suggest that teaching something before the service begins, rather than throwing it in during the time of worship, is the best way to introduce a new song. How many 'new' songs are used needs to be carefully considered too. We are here to lead the peo-

ple to the throne room of God, not to dis-empower them by playing songs they do not know.

Is the worship group representative of the whole of the church? If you find yourself in a situation where teenagers feel dis-empowered in terms of ministry, having some of them in the worship group says to them and their peers that they are part of the church of today, and not the church of tomorrow. This can go both ways and we do well not to only have shiny young people in a worship group. Teenagers to grannies would be an ideal mix but this depends to some degree on whom we are serving and whom we are trying to reach.

How long will the worship leader lead the group and the worship? It may be helpful to discuss with the worship leader exactly how long their season in this area of ministry is likely to last, or at least to put in some length of time after which there will be a period of reflection. It is very easy to give away authority, but much more difficult to ask someone to put down something which they are wedded to.

Who Chooses the Songs?

I have already mentioned my belief that, if we are to release people into ministries, we need to push authority boundaries as much as possible. A church leader may want to have a particular song or hymn, maybe as a link to the sermon or for another good reason, but worship is not about singing the sermon. It is about an encounter with the risen Lord Jesus. The church leader should leave the worship leader to choose the songs as far as possible. It is the worship leader who puts in the prayer and practice. It is the worship leader who should be seeking God's anointing in the music and the group. If church leaders always pick all the songs then the worship group ceases to lead worship and becomes mere accompaniment.

Having said that, there are often good reasons why church leaders want to use certain songs and not others. Good communication and an open working relationship are healthy qualities to nurture between the church leader and worship leader. From the days of the Psalmist, our singing has shaped our theology and practice, so it is important that we remain under authority.

Prophetic gifting

As we rest in the presence of God, he speaks to people in a prophetic way. Church leaders need to pastor this well if the gift is to build up the body. Too often I see the prophets ignored by their church leaders who do not know what to do with them. This causes great pain (both to the prophet and to the body) and may drive prophecy out of the church.[8]

Song Writing

I encourage the worship group to write their own material as well as to play more familiar music. Home grown songs can have a prophetic nature for individual churches and congregations.

One word of warning, though: song writing, like many aspects of being in a worship group, can become a distraction and an excuse to pursue personal glory. My role is to lead the people to the throne of God in worship with the most appropriate material available, not to become the next Graham Kendrick or Matt Redman! Musicians are by nature creative people, but our energies need not be over distracted by looking for the next creative thing in worship.

Multiplying the Ministry

Once a worship group has become established it is important that we grow the ministry and that the established group does not become stale. Many of the battles with choirs and organists in more traditional worship settings happen because there is no sense of the movement of God leading his people into new seasons. When one worship group becomes established, ask the leaders to set up a second. This brings both freedom and variety, and it releases the gifts that God is giving others. I began to teach on worship because I was asked to multiply the ministry. John Wimber actually dismissed one of his worship leaders because he could not do this.

Pastoral Care of the Worship Leader

Finally I need to stress that it is absolutely vital for church leaders to spend time with worship leaders and look after them. Leading worship places someone in a front-line position and they need good pastoral care and line-management. They need to grow as Christians. They need support when they find themselves the focus of complaint, and they need support and guidance when pastoral issues arise in the group. For me personally, knowing that the church leader was there for me and would support me, even when I did something over adventurous, was very liberating.

Questions for Reflection

1   What problems, or potential problems, does your church have in this area?
2   What practicalities could you sort out that would help the group and the church?
3   How do you feel about the use of prophetic and other gifts in worship?
4   How much care do you get? Is it enough?

How We Make the Journey—
Leading as an Individual

7

So far we have concentrated on worship led by a worship group rather than by an individual.

For many of us this is not how we are able to work all of the time. However, the principles are exactly the same when we are leading alone.

To reiterate: if we are wanting to lead worship we need to:

- Plan the direction of our focus to draw people towards God
- Consider the shape of the journey we intend to lead people on
- Encourage people that it is important to worship
- Work on being holy in our leadership
- Plan songs and other elements to enable the journey
- Seek the Lord's anointing
- Deal with any practicalities that might obstruct the journey

All of these are possible, and indeed desirable, when we are working alone. Let us consider some examples.

Small Groups

Leading in a small group is an excellent way of learning to develop our gifting and discovering anointing. A small group of people can be much more encouraging to us and are usually far more forgiving of our mistakes than a larger setting. Importantly too, the intoxicating or terrifying issue of performing in 'public' is much diminished.

A small group also has the huge advantage of having less time constraint than public worship. This means that when we get to rest in the presence of God, we can remain in that place for as long as we feel comfortable. This can sometimes mean an hour or more, which is a luxury not usually afforded to us in congregational worship.

A small group also has the huge advantage of having less time constraint than public worship

Worship by Yourself

In the same way that you can have a time of prayer and Bible study in your own personal devotions, you can also have a time of worship. This can be using a piano or guitar if you are able, or by worshipping along with a CD. Worship, prayer and reading the Bible may then become elements of a whole, rather than individual activities. I think this is essential; worshipping by ourselves equips and sustains us in more public ministry.

An Individual Leading a Congregation—the Spoken Rather than Musical Role

In a normal Anglican setting there is usually someone there to lead the act of worship. Why should we not apply our principles to leading this more formal style of worship? We can, for example, prolong the dialogue towards God by praying either liturgically or spontaneously after singing a hymn. We can leave silent spaces when it is appropriate after any dialogue. In *Common Worship* (the Anglican service book) for example, it is possible to create more of a flow by having the welcome followed by the invitation to confession. It can be harder to sustain momentum in the journey, but when we know what we are aiming for it is much easier to get there!

It is harder to lead charismatic worship alone, but it is certainly not impossible. One of the hardest factors is actually gathering the courage to give it a go. Let me encourage you to find those who will be encouraging and then go for it.

Questions for Reflection

1 How do you worship by yourself?

2 Looking at the 'liturgy' you use, how could you make it more journey oriented?

3 What signs of anointing do you recognize in what you currently do? How could you build on them?

Concluding Remarks 8

Jesus' life demonstrates a very clear pattern of going 'up,',
'in' and 'out.'

He went 'up' to his heavenly Father in worship, 'in' with his disciples in
fellowship, and then 'out' into the world in mission and ministry (see Matthew 28.16–20). I believe that this 'up-in-out' pattern is vital for us to follow
as Christians.

In this life it is worship which comes first and is foundational. The truth of
whom we worship profoundly effects who we are and how we do the works
of the kingdom of God. Our 'up' is crucial to our 'in' and our 'out.' Here I
have described a pattern and highlighted some of what I think is vital to
worship. Let me encourage you to sit down, maybe even now, and work
through some of the questions in this book. What
is important to you as you lead worship? What
journey are you seeking to take people on? How
are you going to do it next time you are called
upon to lead?

*We have only seen a
glimpse of the awesome
power and intimacy we
can experience in the
worship of God*

It is often said that people do not go to church
because they do not believe that they are missing anything. They may well be right. Worship
in which the manifest presence of God is encountered by the worshipper draws both the Christian and the outsider to God.
We have only seen a glimpse of the awesome power and intimacy we can
experience in the worship of God. In worship, however large or small the
numbers of people involved, we encounter the living God, we join God in
his work of calling the people he created, the people he loves, back to himself. There is nothing more important. This worship needs to be faithfully
and carefully led. Let us be bold, let us be adventurous, let us be sensitive
and all the things that we need to be, but let us lead God's people in worship…

'…cos, I don't know about you, but I'm hungry for Jesus!'

Notes

1   Mark Stibbe uses the image of the temple in Jerusalem.

2   David Parker, Emerging Generation conference, New Wine, Hothorpe Hall February 2003.

3   A copy of this sheet can be found in the Online Resources section of the Grove web site, www.grovebooks.co.uk

4   There is much more work to do on the subject of anointing than I have space for here, however I would refer you to an excellent book by R T Kendall called simply *The Anointing* if you wish to explore the subject of anointing further.

5   Kevin Prosch, *Prophetic Worship*, Vineyard Ministries International (Tapes), 1990.

6   See the hymn 'Turn your eyes upon Jesus.'

7   See Frank Lake, *Living in Grace—Spirituality and Ministry* (Acorn Christian Healing Trust, 1994). Lake has also written *Personal Identity: Its Development,* and *Personal Identity: Its Origin,* both published by the Clinical Theology Institute in 1987 which provide valuable resources in this area.

8   There is some excellent teaching on releasing prophetic ministry in church which has been produced by Chris Woods and Bruce Collins at New wine. They encourage learning in a small group. Where people know each other it is usually all right for a prophecy to be spoken out by the person receiving the prophecy. Any dubious prophecies can be accepted because most of those present will recognize that the person giving the prophecy is either new to the gifting and is still learning, or maybe has had too much cheese, but they love them anyway. In a larger group it is better for the one receiving the prophecy to share this with the leader so that there is some sense of 'weighing' by the leader before the prophecy is spoken out. Weighing should still take place in the small group but this is done by everyone present. See Bruce Collins, *Prophecy! A practical guide to develop your prophetic gifting* (New Wine International, 2000).